LET'S DISCUSS

GETTING INTO DRUGS

Pete Sanders and Steve Myers

Franklin Watts
LONDON · SYDNEY

Contents

Designed and produced by
Aladdin Books Ltd
28 Percy Street
London W1P 0LD

First published in
Great Britain in 1996 by
Franklin Watts
96 Leonard Street
London EC2A 4RH

ISBN: 0 7496 2494 9

A catalogue record for this book is available from the British Library.

Printed in Belgium

Designer   Tessa Barwick
Editor   Alex Edmonds
Illustrator   Mike Lacey
Picture   Brooks
Research   Krikler
                Research

Pete Sanders is Senior Lecturer in health education at the University of North London. He was a head teacher for ten years and has written many books on social issues for children.

Steve Myers is a freelance writer who has co-written other titles in this series and worked on several educational projects for children.

The consultant, Julie Johnson is a health education consultant and trainer, working with children and young people, parents, teachers, carers and organisations such as Kidscape.

HOW TO USE THIS BOOK

The books in this series are intended to help young people to understand more about personal issues that may affect their lives. Each book can be read by a child alone, or together with a parent, teacher or helper, so that there is an opportunity to talk through ideas as they come up. Issues raised in the storyline are explored in the accompanying text, inviting further discussion.

At the end of the book there is a section called "What Can We Do?". This section provides practical ideas which will be useful for both young people and adults, as well as a list of the names and addresses of organisations and helplines, providing further information and support.

Introduction

> "My friends were all talking about how great it would be to try drugs. I'm glad I understood how dangerous they could be."

The numbers of young people misusing or abusing drugs is increasing. This book will help you understand why people take drugs, and the effects they can have on their lives. Each chapter introduces a different aspect of the subject, illustrated by a continuing storyline. The characters in the story have to deal with situations which many young people may face. After each episode we stop and discuss the issues raised. By the end you should understand more about the dangers of drug use. You will also understand the ways in which you can ensure that you never develop a problem.

Use, Misuse And Abuse

"I felt so ill that I didn't read the instructions on the packet. I didn't think that just taking an extra couple of paracetamol could be dangerous."

Drugs are powerful chemicals which influence the way in which the body functions. Some drugs can be bought over the counter at chemists or supermarkets. Others are only available on prescription from a doctor. There are also drugs which are made from equally powerful and different chemicals, which are banned substances and are only available illegally.

Drugs only work properly if the person using them follows the instructions. Used incorrectly, drugs can have serious effects on your physical and emotional health.

The effect a drug has depends to a great extent on the person taking it. Factors such as size, sex, fitness – even a person's mood at the time – can all have an influence. The strength, amount and frequency of use will also have an effect. You misuse a drug that you buy over the counter or get from a doctor if you take it in the wrong dosage or at the wrong times (or with other drugs, thereby making it unsafe). Drug abuse means taking a drug or other chemical for a different purpose to the one it was meant for, in the wrong amount or by the wrong method. Because many drugs prescribed by doctors are very strong, their possession and use are controlled by law.

Use, Misuse And Abuse

▽ Susan Pearson had a migraine, and couldn't take part in her school's sports day.

IT'S NOT FAIR. I'VE BEEN LOOKING FORWARD TO IT FOR AGES.

ARE YOU SURE YOU DON'T WANT A PAINKILLER. JUST THIS ONCE?

YOU KNOW SHE WON'T, MUM. SHE'S INTO ALL THIS ALTERNATIVE MEDICINE STUFF. IT DOESN'T SEEM TO BE WORKING, THOUGH.

SHOWS WHAT YOU KNOW. AND THEY'RE NOT ALTERNATIVES – SOME OF THESE HERBAL CURES HAVE BEEN AROUND FOR YEARS. YOU SHOULD TRY IT INSTEAD OF REACHING FOR A PILL BOTTLE WHENEVER YOU FEEL ROUGH.

NO ARGUING, YOU TWO. PHILIP, YOU'D BETTER GET A MOVE ON. YOU'LL BE LATE FOR YOUR OWN EVENT.

THIS IS ONLY SCHOOL STUFF. IT'S THE CLUB TRIALS THAT REALLY MATTER.

△ Philip belonged to his local athletics club, and was one of its star runners.

GOOD RACE. I WASN'T THAT FAR BEHIND YOU THIS TIME, THOUGH. ONE OF THESE DAYS I'LL BEAT YOU.

IN YOUR DREAMS. HEY, MICHAEL, WE'RE GOING TO GO TO GET SOMETHING TO EAT AFTERWARDS. DO YOU WANT TO COME WITH US?

I THOUGHT YOU WERE USING A LOT OF THAT STUFF. THIS MUST BE SERIOUS. WHAT IS IT NOW? TWO WHOLE WEEKS?

YOU'RE SO FUNNY. YOU'RE BOTH JUST JEALOUS. SOPHIE'S REALLY NICE – SHE'S A REAL LAUGH.

THANKS, BUT I CAN'T. I'M MEETING SOPHIE. WE'RE GOING TO THE CINEMA.

SHE'D HAVE TO BE TO GO OUT WITH YOU! I'M NOT JEALOUS. I'M TOO BUSY TRAINING TO BOTHER WITH GIRLFRIENDS.

▽ Susan was back at school a couple of days later.

KELLY, WHAT ARE YOU DOING?

I THINK MY GLANDS ARE SWOLLEN. I'M COMING DOWN WITH SOMETHING, I'M SURE.

IT'S OKAY. MICHAEL HAD THE SAME THING LAST WEEK. THE DOCTOR GAVE HIM SOME ANTIBIOTICS. I THINK THERE ARE STILL SOME LEFT. I'LL TAKE ONE WHEN I GET HOME.

DON'T BE STUPID. THAT'S DANGEROUS. YOU SHOULD NEVER TAKE PILLS THAT ARE PRESCRIBED FOR SOMEONE ELSE – EVEN YOUR BROTHER.

TRACEY'S RIGHT. YOU DON'T EVEN KNOW FOR SURE IT'S THE SAME THING.

YOU SHOULD TRY GARLIC CAPSULES, THEY'RE GREAT FOR THAT KIND OF THING. SERIOUSLY, BRIAN. IT'S TRUE.

△ Kelly decided not to take the pills.

Some athletes believe that steroids improve performance.

ALCOHOL

Alcohol is very addictive. It is legal in most countries but with age limits.

EFFECTS – Alcohol will often have a relaxing effect, but if too much is consumed, people become 'drunk' and lose control.

SIDE EFFECTS – Too much alcohol causes a mixture of nausea, headaches and trembling commonly known as a 'hangover'. Alcohol also causes serious diseases, including liver damage, damage to the nervous system and heart disease. A lot of people die each year from alcohol-related diseases, such as liver failure.

CANNABIS

Cannabis is illegal in most countries, and it is the most commonly used illegal drug in Britain. It is obtained from the hemp plant, and it is usually smoked. Illegal cannabis is produced in three forms: marijuana, which is a dried tobacco-like substance; cannabis resin, which is commonly called hashish or hash; and cannabis oil or hash oil, which is the liquid form.

EFFECTS – Feelings of joyfulness, recklessness and over-confidence often result.

SIDE EFFECTS – High doses may produce nausea, diarrhoea and vomiting. Feelings of panic and paranoia may be experienced with high doses or after prolonged use. If the user is nervous or depressed these unpleasant feelings may grow worse.

STREET NAMES – pot, hash, dope, grass and ganga.

COCAINE

A powerful stimulant, cocaine is a fluffy white powder which sometimes looks like snow flakes. It is inhaled. Crack is a form of cocaine. It is illegal to possess or sell cocaine.

EFFECTS – People feel more alert and may feel aggressive after taking cocaine.

SIDE EFFECTS – Cocaine damages the nose. It also results in serious weight loss. Crack is especially addictive.

STREET NAMES – Cocaine is called coke, snow or toot. Crack is often called freebase.

ECSTASY

Ecstasy is often called the 'love drug', as it is said to promote feelings of closeness between people. It is illegal to possess or sell ecstasy. It is used widely by young people who are into the rave scene.

Its appearance varies. The tablets may be brown or white, or come in coloured capsules.

EFFECTS – The effects can depend on the amount taken and the mood of the user. They include sweating, dry mouth, tight jaw, high blood pressure and high energy.

SIDE EFFECTS – People feel nauseous and unsteady. Over a period of time anxiety, depression, panic, insomnia and mental health problems may develop. It also causes liver and kidney damage. There have been several deaths from esctasy use.

STREET NAMES – E, XTC.

HEROIN

Heroin is obtained from opium poppies and is usually a brownish powder. It can be dissolved and injected, or smoked. Injecting drugs is more dangerous, as the drug goes immediately into the bloodstream. It is illegal to possess or sell heroin. It is very addictive.

EFFECTS – Heroin gives the user a feeling of intense well-being when it is first used, but this will change very quickly, and the withdrawal feelings may be very painful, causing vomiting, aches and tiredness.

SIDE EFFECTS – Dangers are from overdose or from impurities such as bleach, which may be mixed with the drugs when they are sold.

STREET NAMES – Often called smack, skag or H.

LSD

LSD comes in many forms, often pressed into paper, with designs on, or as tiny tablets or gelatine squares. It is illegal to possess or sell LSD.

EFFECTS – People often 'see things', feel confused and possibly very vulnerable.

SIDE EFFECTS – LSD causes

extreme moods. Flashbacks occur several months after use. It is easy to overdose on.

STREET NAMES – Acid, trips, Lucy, or by the description of the design on the paper.

SOLVENTS

Glue, varnishes and lighter fluid can all be inhaled. It is against the law for a shop to sell solvents if they suspect they will be sniffed.

EFFECTS – They give a feeling of well-being and dizziness.

SIDE EFFECTS – Nausea, tiredness and headaches can occur. Sniffing solvents can cause death, through inhaling vomit or a lack of oxygen.

TOBACCO

Tobacco is made from a leaf formed into cigarettes or cigars. Nicotine in tobacco smoke can cause cancer. It is illegal for people below a certain age to be sold cigarettes.

EFFECTS – Tobacco is habit-forming and very addictive.

SIDE EFFECTS – Cancer and heart disease can be caused by smoking.

—3— *Getting Into Drugs*

"I just thought it would be a bit of fun, but before I knew it I was doing drugs all the time, and then found that I couldn't stop."

Most people use drugs and medicines correctly. Some, however, look to drugs for more than help with health problems. They may believe taking drugs, like tranquilizers, provides an escape from pain or difficult situations. Others take drugs, such as steroids, to enhance performance – in sport or stressful situations. Many people abuse drugs as a form of rebellion or through boredom. Or because others are doing it. Some people do it simply because they want to.

Doctors have sometimes been criticised for allowing people to continue repeating the same prescription for drugs without making sure that the patient still needs the drug to help with a problem. Because people are so used to being given drugs to cure physical illnesses, they may look to drugs to help them with difficult feelings or moods. Perhaps they hope that it will make them happier. Although drugs may allow people to blot out unhappy thoughts or situations, they only provide temporary relief. Taking drugs does not solve problems – worries will still be there once the effect of the drug has worn off. There are lots of other ways to cope with stressful situations or cope with boredom, such as taking exercise or listening to music.

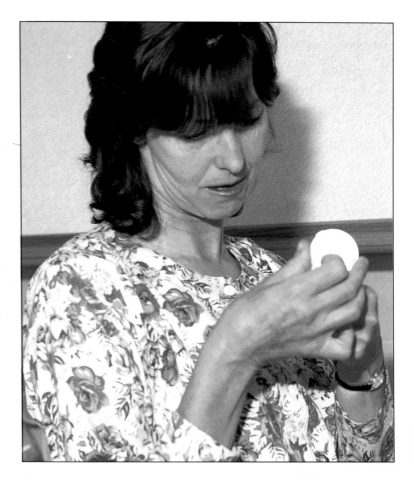

Some people have come to rely on drugs because doctors give them repeat prescriptions they don't need.

Getting Into Drugs

▽ One evening, Philip and Bruno ran into Michael.

HI, GUYS. THIS IS SOPHIE.

GOOD TO MEET YOU, SOPHIE. MICHAEL, HOW COME YOU'RE SMOKING?

YEAH, A MONTH AGO YOU WERE SAYING WHAT A DISGUSTING HABIT IT IS.

▽ Michael said he had changed his mind. He'd started because Sophie smoked.

I LIKE IT. I THINK IT MAKES YOU LOOK SOPHISTICATED.

I DON'T SEE WHAT'S SO SOPHISTICATED ABOUT DOING SOMETHING THAT CAN CAUSE CANCER AND HEART DISEASE, NOT TO MENTION MAKING YOUR BREATH SMELL!

I THINK YOU MADE YOUR POINT, BRUNO! WHERE ARE YOU TWO OFF TO ANYWAY?

IT'S THIS PLACE A FRIEND OF SOPHIE'S HEARD ABOUT, IT SOUNDS LIKE A GREAT NIGHT.

JANINE USUALLY FINDS THE WILD EVENTS. YOU SHOULD COME ALONG.

THANKS, BUT COUNT ME OUT. I'VE GOT TRAINING TOMORROW AND COACH IS ALREADY ON AT ME TO IMPROVE MY TIMINGS.

▽ When they arrived, Sophie went to find Janine.

DID YOU HAVE ENOUGH MONEY? DID YOU MANAGE TO GET SOME?

SURE DID. HERE, TAKE YOUR SHARE BEFORE ANYONE SEES US.

▽ Janine had given Sophie four tabs of Ecstasy. Michael was shocked.

ALL MY FRIENDS DO IT. I'VE TRIED A COUPLE OF OTHER THINGS TOO. I LIKE TO GET HIGH. TRY SOME.

NO THANKS. I DIDN'T KNOW YOU USED THAT STUFF.

▽ A week later, Philip was beaten in an important race.

I CAN'T BELIEVE I LOST. I PUT IN SO MUCH TRAINING. COACH MADE ME FEEL LIKE I'D LET THE WHOLE CLUB DOWN.

THAT GUY'S A REAL PAIN. SO YOU LOST, HUH?

WHAT ARE YOU DOING HERE? ANYWAY, AT LEAST PHILIP DIDN'T CHEAT TO WIN.

9

Getting Into Drugs

Drugs can affect all aspects of your life. They could even kill you.

TRACEY AND BRIAN WERE KEEN TO TRY ALCOHOL.

Often when you are growing up, the excitement of trying out new things and new experiences can be very strong. Experimenting is a very normal part of growing up, but you should try not to expose yourself to unnecessary risks. If you want to try drugs, or have already tried them (even if you had no ill effects) you need to think very carefully about what could happen. Any advantages of taking drugs are far outweighed by the dangers they can pose to your health, your happiness and your relationships.

BRUNO WAS SHOCKED TO DISCOVER MICHAEL HAD TAKEN UP SMOKING.

Below a certain age it is illegal for you to buy alcohol, and for shops to sell you cigarettes. However, alcohol and cigarettes are not restricted in the way many other drugs are. It is easy to forget that the substances in them are very powerful indeed. More people die each year from using or abusing tobacco and alcohol than any other kinds of drugs.

SOPHIE THINKS THAT TAKING ECSTASY IS OKAY.

Often people have an image of illegal drug use as being exciting. In fact, the reality of drug abuse is often very different from the image.

Coping With Pressures

Relationships with other people can be some of the most important influences on your life and the choices you make. Sometimes pressure from others can be a factor in people's decisions to abuse drugs. They may want to be accepted by a particular group or be afraid of not being respected if they refuse to go along with them. Or they might think taking drugs will give them a reputation as a rebel and make others look up to them.

It is important not to let your desire to be part of a group interfere with your ability to make responsible and sensible decisions about your life and health.

Coping with pressures from those around you, especially schoolfriends or other people your age, is not always easy. Many will use unfair tactics to persuade people to act in a certain way – such as trying to make you look stupid or attempting to convince you that everyone does it. Gangs in particular might demand loyalty from their members, and this can make it difficult to get your own views and opinions heard. Although it can be hard to stand up to these pressures, it is important to remember the possible consequences of drug abuse – not only on you but also on those close to you.

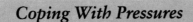

▽ The next day, Tracey did not go to school.

TRACEY'S STILL REALLY ILL AND I CAN'T REMEMBER THE PARTY AT ALL. MUM AND DAD ARE STILL REALLY ANGRY.

YOU WERE REALLY DRUNK. YOU MUST HAVE KNOWN YOUR DAD WOULD SEE.

I KNOW - AND LOTS OF THEM DRINK TOO MUCH.

OH, COME ON SUSAN. YOU'RE AS BAD AS MY PARENTS. ADULTS ARE ALWAYS TELLING US WHAT'S GOOD FOR US AND BAD FOR US. BUT THEY DRINK AND SMOKE.

LEAVE HIM ALONE, SUSAN. IT WAS ONLY A BIT OF FUN. LOADS OF PEOPLE DRINK.

WE DON'T DRINK ALCOHOL BECAUSE OF OUR RELIGION. I'M TEMPTED TO TRY IT SOMETIMES, THOUGH.

△ Brian said he had thought drinking would make him feel really good.

I DON'T NEED THIS HANGOVER, IT'S JUST NOT WORTH IT.

IT'S UP TO YOU WHAT YOU DO, BUT BOOZE AND CIGGIES CAN CAUSE SO MANY ILLNESSES. AND ADULTS ARE AT RISK TOO.

▽ Two weeks later, Philip was still having trouble with his running times.

THAT WAS BETTER, PHIL, BUT NOT THE BEST YOU'VE EVER DONE.

I'M GOING TO DO THIS. I WANT TO MAKE THE REGIONAL FINALS. HEY, MICHAEL, WHY AREN'T YOU RUNNING TODAY?

MICHAEL'S TAKEN UP SMOKING, AND I'VE TRIED IT. I DIDN'T LIKE IT MUCH, THOUGH. I MIGHT TRY AGAIN SOME DAY.

I HAD A LATE NIGHT LAST NIGHT. I WAS WITH SOPHIE AND HER FRIENDS AGAIN.

△ The four of them went into class still discussing it.

▽ Philip was fed up about his training. Two days later, he decided to go and see Marty.

THEY'RE A BIT WILD. I TRIED ECSTASY FOR THE FIRST TIME YESTERDAY. IT GAVE ME QUITE A BUZZ.

MICHAEL, YOU SHOULD BE CAREFUL! THAT STUFF CAN BE REALLY DANGEROUS.

I'VE BEEN THINKING ABOUT WHAT YOU SAID ABOUT A TRAINING SHORTCUT. WOULD YOU BE ABLE TO GET ME SOMETHING LIKE YOU HAD?

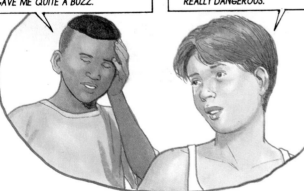

△ Michael said he knew what he was doing.

WELL YOU'VE CHANGED YOUR TUNE. THERE'S NOTHING LIKE THE DESIRE FOR VICTORY IS THERE? SURE, I CAN GET YOU SOMETHING, BUT IT'LL COST YOU. MEET ME HERE AGAIN TOMORROW.

YOU ARE AN INDIVIDUAL, AND YOU MAKE YOUR OWN DECISIONS.

No matter how much pressure those around you are putting on you to go along with them, remember that you have the right to say no. Refusing to get involved with illegal drug use does not make you weak or a coward. It shows that you are not prepared to take unnecessary risks with your health or become involved in something where you could end up breaking the law.

KELLY AND THE OTHERS HAVE DIFFERING VIEWS ON CERTAIN ISSUES.

Puberty is the process your body undergoes to change you from a child to a young adult. During this period, you might find yourself in conflict with friends, or having constantly changing moods. This is because of the increased amounts of certain chemicals in your bloodstream. Try not to let mood swings influence you into making decisions you might regret.

CASE STUDY: CAMILLA, AGED 15

"I realise now it's not enough to know about the dangers. You have to understand how to protect yourself. I knew all the risks, but I was with this crowd of people who were all taking drugs and daring me to try. Instead of just walking away, I took a tablet. I didn't even know what it was! I had a bad reaction – I lost control and I couldn't tell what was going on. It was scary. It was my decision, and it was a bad one. I'll never do it again."

14

Highs And Lows

"I used to have a good bunch of friends. Once I got into the drug scene, I was always so tired from all the partying, and from the drug effects that I didn't care about anyone else at all."

Most people who abuse drugs believe they can control what they are doing. Initially they may want the 'high' they think the drug will give them. This can be a feeling of pleasure or happiness. Or they might be looking to drugs to give them extra energy. But the down side of drug misuse can be very serious indeed. Drugs can cost you your health and spoil your chances for the future.

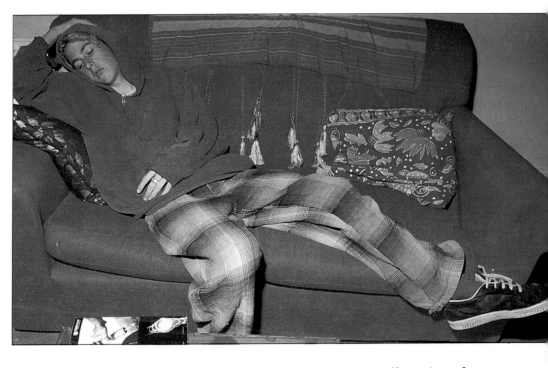

Once people are involved with drugs, many of them stop caring about their appearance and lose interest in their friends.

People may believe that taking drugs makes them a more interesting person. Drugs can seriously alter a person's behaviour. Someone who is normally a calm person might suddenly lose control, and do things which he or she would never normally do. Possession and supply of certain drugs is an offence, and some people end up with a criminal record, which may affect their future prospects. For instance, if you have a criminal record you can't join the police or become a nurse. Also, the effects of a drug overdose can be fatal – people have died because they have taken too much of a drug, or because it was too strong, too pure or mixed with something that was poisonous.

▽ Three months later. Philip had been taking steroids regularly, and his performance had improved.

WE'RE REALLY PROUD OF YOU PHILIP. WELL DONE. YOU'RE GOING TO BE IN THE REGIONAL FINALS.

THAT WAS A GREAT RACE, SON. YOU SEE, I TOLD YOU ALL THAT TRAINING WOULD EVENTUALLY PAY OFF.

THERE'LL BE A LOT OF GOOD RUNNERS THERE, THOUGH. I CAN'T AFFORD TO LET UP NOW.

▽ One evening, Michael called for Sophie.

WHAT DO YOU WANT TO DO? FANCY THE CINEMA?

LET'S SCORE SOME DRUGS, I REALLY FEEL LIKE GETTING OUT OF IT.

YOU'VE CHANGED, YOU KNOW. THAT'S ALL YOU EVER THINK ABOUT THESE DAYS. WHY DO WE HAVE TO GET HIGH ALL THE TIME? I DON'T FEEL GOOD AFTERWARDS. WE USED TO HAVE FUN. NOW ALL WE DO IS GET STONED.

OH, COME ON, MICHAEL. PLEASE. I REALLY NEED SOMETHING.

▽ The next morning, Kelly went to wake up Michael.

HEY, MICHAEL, YOU'RE GOING TO BE LATE. BOY, YOU LOOK AWFUL.

THANKS A LOT. I WAS OUT LATE LAST NIGHT. I WA... WITH SOPHIE - I'M TRYING TO REMEMBER WHER... WE WENT, AND HOW I MANAGED TO GET HOME.

△ In the end, Michael went along with her.

MICHAEL ARE YOU TAKING SOMETHING? I KNOW YOU'VE STARTED SMOKING, AND YOU'VE BEEN ACTING WEIRD LATELY.

I'M O.K. I'VE EXPERIMENTED WITH A COUPLE OF THINGS. DON'T YOU TELL MUM AND DAD. I'LL BE FINE.

I'M WORRIED ABOUT YOU. YOU'VE BEEN DIFFERENT SINCE YOU STARTED GOING OUT WITH THAT SOPHIE.

I LIKE HER. SHE'S FUN, BUT SHE'S GOT INVOLVED TOO HEAVILY WITH THIS DRUGS THING. I ONLY TRIED IT BECAUSE I DIDN'T WANT HER TO GO OFF ME.

MICHAEL STILL BELIEVES HE IS IN CONTROL OF THE SITUATION WITH HIM AND SOPHIE.

Many young people, who are fully aware of the dangers of drugs, often refuse to accept that they are putting themselves at risk. It can be tempting to think 'it won't happen to me'. The truth, however, is very different. There is no one type of person who becomes a drug abuser. It can and does happen to anyone. The only way to be sure you do not develop a problem is not to take drugs in the first place.

MICHAEL CAN'T REMEMBER THE PREVIOUS EVENING.

The effects of some drugs on the brain can seriously damage your memory and your ability to think. Many people have found themselves in situations of a sexual or criminal nature, which, had it not been for the effect of drugs, they would not have become involved in.

FACTFILE:
ADDICTION

- Continued use of certain drugs can lead to a person becoming addicted to the effects of the drug.
- The body can become tolerant to the effects of a drug, which means that the person has to take increasingly larger doses to achieve the same effect.
- There are two types of addiction: People can become physically addicted to a drug, meaning that their body craves the drug in order to function. Or they can be psychologically addicted to it, which means they believe that they will not be able to carry out certain ordinary tasks unless they have the drug inside them.

—6— Supply And Demand

As long as suppliers can earn money from them, they will encourage people to misuse or abuse drugs. Suppliers – sometimes called dealers or pushers – may have different reasons for doing what they do. Some work for other people; others do it purely for their own gain. Some suppliers are drug abusers themselves and sell drugs to get the money they need to buy their own.

Often suppliers may be friends or acquaintances of the user, and believe that they are doing him or her a favour. Professional suppliers may often come across as being very friendly initially, until they have built up a solid relationship and are sure that a person is dependent upon them for their supply of drugs. No matter how pleasant or caring these kinds of suppliers might seem at first, their main aim is to make money. They do not care whether a person can afford to pay, and many might even become violent if someone cannot clear a debt. Although suppliers may have access to large amounts of illegal drugs, they do not usually have any control over the quality of them. These drugs are not screened to make sure they are safe, and many are 'cut' – mixed with other substances to make the drugs go further so that they make yet more money.

Even if a dealer is someone you know, you cannot be sure that what he or she is giving you will be the same every time.

Supply And Demand

▽ That Friday, Philip went to his regular meeting with Marty.

> SORRY PHIL. THAT'S NOT ENOUGH ANY MORE. THIS STUFF'S NOT EASY TO GET HOLD OF, YOU KNOW. I'M GOING TO NEED DOUBLE IN FUTURE.

> GIVE ME A BREAK, MARTY. I'VE ALREADY GIVEN YOU ALL MY SAVINGS, WHERE AM I GOING TO GET MORE?

> THAT'S NOT MY PROBLEM IS IT? HEY, LOOK, PHIL, I'M DOING YOU A FAVOUR HERE. OF COURSE, IF YOU DON'T WANT THE STUFF...

> NO, I WANT IT. IT'S HELPING ME - THE FINALS ARE ONLY A MONTH AWAY NOW. I'LL GET SOME MONEY SOMEHOW. MEET ME AGAIN TOMORROW.

▽ The next evening, Susan caught her brother going through their Mum's handbag.

> OH, HI THERE. I WAS JUST LOOKING FOR THAT LETTER GRAN SENT. I THOUGHT I MIGHT WRITE TO HER.

> YOU? WRITE A LETTER? GIVE ME A BREAK. WHAT'S GOING ON? YOU'VE BEEN ON EDGE ALL DAY.

△ Marty agreed, and Philip left, wondering what he was going to do.

> I'M NERVOUS ABOUT THE FINALS, THAT'S ALL. I THOUGHT WRITING MIGHT HELP ME TO CALM DOWN.

> THEY'RE AGES AWAY YET. AND YOUR TRAINING'S GOING REALLY WELL. OH WELL, SUIT YOURSELF.

△ Susan left, and Philip slipped the money he had just stolen from his mum's purse into his pocket.

▽ That evening, Philip met Marty again.

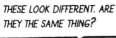

> THESE LOOK DIFFERENT. ARE THEY THE SAME THING?

> I TOLD YOU, THEY'RE NOT THAT EASY TO COME BY. THE GUY I GOT THEM FROM HAD TO GO SOMEWHERE ELSE THIS TIME. YOU'LL BE FINE WITH THESE. TRUST ME.

> WE SAW PHILIP ON SATURDAY, DOWN BY THE ARCADE. HE WAS WITH MARTY.

> MARTY? WHAT WOULD PHILIP BE DOING TALKING TO HIM?

> I DON'T KNOW, BUT THEY LOOKED PRETTY FRIENDLY.

△ Susan said they must have made a mistake. Philip hadn't been friends with Marty for ages.

MARTY HAS TOLD PHILIP HE WILL HAVE TO PAY MORE FOR THE DRUGS.

Suppliers will often use this tactic to get more money out of their customers. Initially, they might offer drugs at a very low price in order to get a person interested. But once that person has become hooked on the drug, prices will often rise.

SOME PEOPLE BELIEVE THAT SUPPLYING CAN BE A WAY TO MAKE MONEY QUICKLY.

These people often forget, or choose to ignore, the fact that the money is being made through an activity which causes misery and distress for so many people. They affect not only the health – and

perhaps the life – of others, but are engaging in a criminal activity and risk ruining their self-esteem.

PHILIP WONDERED WHY THE DRUGS MARTY GAVE HIM LOOKED DIFFERENT.

One of the dangers with drugs is that you can never be sure whether what you think you are getting is actually what you are buying. There are many types of similar drugs, which might have very different effects. In addition, most suppliers are not worried about what they sell. It could be a different drug altogether, or a different strength or may have been mixed with a poisonous substance.

Drugs And The Law

All drugs are controlled under the law. However, the laws are not the same for all drugs.

Some drugs are allowed to be sold to the general public in chemists and supermarkets. Others can only be prescribed by doctors. Use of drugs like nicotine and alcohol is permitted, but they can only be bought once a person has reached a particular age. Other substances which are misused, such as glue and other solvents, might also have an age restriction. Certain drugs are completely prohibited.

Some people believe that possession and use of certain drugs should be legalised. Others think that would just make the situation much worse. Many believe that some of the laws aren't very clear. For instance, in many countries, although it is illegal for a child to buy alcohol from a shop, it is not illegal for a child to drink alcohol. The laws in some countries used to be quite relaxed about the possession of drugs such as cannabis. Recently, in countries such as Holland, the laws relating to this drug have been tightened. In most places it is still illegal to possess these drugs. Drugs such as heroin, cocaine, speed and ecstasy are prohibited everywhere. Convictions for possession of these kinds of drug can carry very heavy fines and long prison sentences. Remember that even legal drugs are not harmless. If used incorrectly any drug can be dangerous.

Police in most countries can search anyone they believe may possess an illegal drug.

▽ Next month, Philip won the regional finals.

THAT WAS BRILLIANT, PHILIP. YOU FLEW DOWN THAT TRACK. HEY, WHAT'S WRONG?

I JUST FEEL A BIT DIZZY. TOO HOT. I THINK I NEED TO SIT DOWN FOR A MINUTE.

▽ But before he could get to the bench, he collapsed.

WHAT'S WRONG WITH HIM?

I DON'T KNOW. GIVE HIM SOME ROOM. PHILIP? PHILIP? OKAY, BRUNO, GET AN AMBULANCE.

▽ At the hospital, Philip's parents waited for news. Coach arrived with his things.

WHAT'S GOING ON? THEY PHONED US AND SAID THAT PHILIP HAD COLLAPSED.

THAT CAN'T BE RIGHT. PHILIP WOULDN'T DO SOMETHING LIKE THAT. WOULD HE?

HE DID. I THINK I KNOW WHY. I WAS SORTING HIS THINGS OUT, AND CAME ACROSS THESE IN HIS BAG. I THINK PHILIP'S BEEN TAKING STEROIDS. WE MUST TELL THE DOCTORS ABOUT THIS.

▽ Later, Kelly was talking to Michael.

I SAW SUSAN TODAY. SHE SAYS PHILIP'S OUT OF DANGER.

THANK GOODNESS. I CAN'T BELIEVE HE CHEATED LIKE THAT. HE WAS REALLY STUPID TAKING THOSE THINGS.

THAT COULD HAVE BEEN YOU, THOUGH, MICHAEL. I KNOW YOU'RE STILL ON DRUGS. YOU'RE GOING TO BE IN SERIOUS TROUBLE. WHY WON'T YOU TELL MUM AND DAD WHAT'S GOING ON? THEY COULD HELP.

I CAN HANDLE IT, KELLY. DON'T YOU DARE MENTION THIS TO THEM. I'LL SORT IT OUT IN MY OWN WAY.

▽ The next night, Sophie had some bad news.

MICHAEL, IT'S AWFUL. JANINE'S BEEN ARRESTED. SHE'S GOING TO BE CHARGED WITH POSSESSING DRUGS.

I KNEW THIS WOULD HAPPEN. WE'VE GOT TO STOP THIS, SOPHIE. IT'S ILLEGAL AND IT'S MESSING US UP. YOU'VE REALLY CHANGED. IF YOU WON'T DO SOMETHING, THEN I DON'T WANT TO BE AROUND YOU ANY MORE. I'M SORRY, SOPHIE.

△ But Michael knew things were getting out of hand.

MANY PEOPLE FIND THEMSELVES COMMITTING OTHER CRIMES TO PAY FOR A DRUG HABIT.

Illegal drugs are expensive. People find that their money soon runs out. Some drug users have turned to theft, mugging or prostitution to get money to pay for the drugs. People can be so influenced by the effect of the drug or the addiction to it, that they don't care about anything else.

THE MAJORITY OF LAWS ARE CREATED TO PROTECT PEOPLE'S RIGHTS, WELL-BEING AND PROPERTY.

Many rules and regulations can seem unfair when you are growing up, especially if you believe they are

CASE STUDY: DAVID, AGED 15

"I knew some of my friends were taking drugs, but I was determined not to do it myself. I needed money, though, and I thought selling drugs would be a good way of raising it. I wasn't a big-time supplier. I just got drugs for a few friends. Then the police caught me with some marijuana and ecstasy. I was arrested and taken to the police station. They charged me with possession and supplying. Now I have a criminal record, and some of my friends don't want to know me any more. I thought they'd stick by me."

restricting your freedom. You might not be able to see the point of some of them, or believe that you should not have to take notice of others. Very few rules are created without a good reason – even if that reason isn't immediately obvious. You cannot just ignore the law without being prepared to face the consequences of what you are doing.

Getting Help

"The most difficult step for me was admitting to myself that I had a problem. I couldn't do anything until I'd faced that fact."

Drug abuse can have very serious effects on people's lives. The good news, however, is that there is a great deal of help available for those with a problem. Nobody intends to develop a drug habit. Those who do might find it difficult to come off drugs, and it may take a long while for people to completely beat their addiction. Even those who are not dependent upon the drugs might find it hard to change their behaviour. There are many ways to begin to combat a drug problem.

Talking about a drug problem with others who are going through the same thing can help you realise that you are not alone with the problem, and that drug addiction can be beaten.

How difficult it is to quit drug-taking will often depend on how long a person has been taking drugs and how dependent they have become. Some people may need a great deal of support or treatment to overcome their problem – they may even need to spend time in hospital. Coming off a drug immediately may not be possible for some – it may even be dangerous if their body has become so used to the effects. Doctors may decide to substitute a different drug or a lower strength, to gradually help a person beat the addiction. The important thing is to realise you have a problem and get the right kind of help for you.

▽ Philip made a good recovery, though the doctors said he might have died.

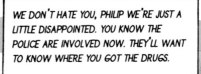
WE DON'T HATE YOU, PHILIP WE'RE JUST A LITTLE DISAPPOINTED. YOU KNOW THE POLICE ARE INVOLVED NOW. THEY'LL WANT TO KNOW WHERE YOU GOT THE DRUGS.

YOUR COACH WAS REALLY ANGRY. YOU KNOW OF COURSE THAT THE RESULT WON'T STAND. YOU'VE BEEN DISQUALIFIED. WHY DID YOU DO IT, PHILIP?

I JUST WANTED TO WIN SO MUCH. I WANTED EVERYONE TO BE PROUD OF ME. NOW EVERYONE HATES ME.

OH NO, MUM. I CAN'T TELL THEM.

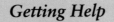

YOU DON'T HAVE TO. IT WAS MARTY WASN'T IT? TRACEY AND BRIAN SAW YOU WITH HIM. HE'D KNOW WHERE TO GET THE STUFF.

△ His mum said he must get well and start to put the whole episode behind him.

▽ Michael had decided to tell his parents what was going on.

I DON'T KNOW WHAT TO SAY, MICHAEL. I THOUGHT YOU KNEW ABOUT THE DANGERS OF DRUGS. WHAT WERE YOU THINKING ABOUT? AND WHERE DID YOU GET THE MONEY FROM TO BUY THEM?

I'M SO SORRY. I THOUGHT I COULD KEEP IT UNDER CONTROL, BUT I CAN'T. I REALLY NEED YOUR HELP.

SOPHIE HAD MOST OF THE MONEY – HER PARENTS ARE LOADED. SHE'S IN A WORSE STATE THAN I AM. I SPENT ALL MY ALLOWANCE, THOUGH. I FEEL LIKE I'VE RUINED EVERYTHING. I'VE STOPPED TRAINING, MY SCHOOLWORK'S SUFFERED...

WHAT'S SOPHIE GOING TO DO?

THAT'S NOT IMPORTANT RIGHT NOW. HE'S TOLD US ABOUT IT AND HE WANTS OUR HELP. DON'T WORRY, MICHAEL WE'LL GET THROUGH THIS.

△ Michael said he wasn't seeing her any more.

▽ The next evening, however, Michael had a visitor.

HI. I JUST WANTED TO SAY I'M SORRY. YOU WERE RIGHT. I'M A MESS, MICHAEL. I DO NEED HELP, BUT I DON'T KNOW WHAT TO DO. I CAN'T TALK TO MY DAD – HE'S AWAY ALL THE TIME, AND MUM WOULD JUST GO SPARE. I THINK IT'S TOO LATE.

NO IT'S NOT. LOOK I'VE TOLD MY PARENTS EVERYTHING.

WE RANG A HELPLINE AND THEY GAVE US SOME GOOD ADVICE AND THE NAME OF A COUNSELLING GROUP I CAN GO TO. WHY DON'T YOU COME ALONG? AT LEAST PHONE THE HELPLINE IF YOU CAN'T TALK TO ANYONE ELSE. PLEASE, SOPHIE.

◁ Sophie said she'd think about it.

dependence can be tackled with the right support and commitment. If you just leave a problem, it will never be solved.

NOBODY PRETENDS THAT OVERCOMING A DRUG PROBLEM WILL BE EASY.

The craving may last a long time, and some people are tempted back to drugs, and may try several times before they can really kick their habit. The more help and support they receive from those around them, the easier it will be. But the most important factor is the determination to beat the dependence.

MICHAEL TOLD SOPHIE THAT IT'S NEVER TOO LATE TO GET HELP WITH A DRUG PROBLEM.

It may not be easy, but it is worth it. Often people are afraid to ask for help, because they think things have gone too far. They may see the situation as hopeless. Obviously, the earlier you start, the easier it is to overcome, but all kinds of drug

FACTFILE:
MAKING THE FIRST MOVE

- Believing in yourself is a very important factor.
- Don't put off a decision to get help. Sometimes people only seek help after they've already had a bad experience.
- You don't have to wait until you've already developed a problem to ask for help. If you are thinking of taking drugs, talk to someone about your feelings.
- It can be difficult to challenge someone you care about and make him or her see the problem, but sometimes other people might have to make the first move.
- Finding the right kind of help is vital. Your own doctor might be the first person to call on. Or if you prefer someone not directly involved, there are many organisations which can provide advice.

Being Yourself

"I realised that the person I was when I was taking drugs wasn't really me. That was someone I didn't like very much and couldn't control."

Self esteem – a belief in your own self worth – is important throughout your life. It doesn't just happen though, and you may face difficult situations and comments from others which threaten how you feel about yourself. Finding your own identity as you grow up is not always easy. You are likely to experience conflicting feelings and messages, and making sense of your emotions may sometimes be difficult.

Nobody should need to take drugs to have a good time.

Some people take drugs because they think the drugs help them to handle difficult situations. Or they may have a very low self image and believe that the drugs will make them more interesting or give them a way of escaping from their feelings. Often these young people begin by sniffing glue or other solvents, and may go on to other drugs later. Not everyone who takes drugs has low self esteem. Some do it simply because they want to know what will happen – or because they think that none of the bad effects of drug use will happen to them. These people are ignoring the real risks of the situation.

▽ Two months later Philip ran into Bruno in town.

> OH HI. I WAS JUST OFF TO THE CLUB. I DIDN'T EXPECT TO SEE YOU.

> HOW HAVE YOU BEEN? LOOK I KNOW YOU HAD THE RIGHT TO BE ANGRY WITH ME BEFORE. AND I'M SORRY I CHEATED. BUT I'D STILL LIKE TO BE MATES.

▽ He and Bruno had had a huge row, and hadn't spoken properly since.

> I DIDN'T WANT TO FALL OUT ANY MORE THAN YOU DID. BUT YOU LET US ALL DOWN. WHAT HAPPENED WITH THE POLICE?

> THEY'RE NOT GOING TO PRESS CHARGES AGAINST ME. BUT MARTY'S BEEN CHARGED WITH SUPPLYING. THEY ACTUALLY CAUGHT HIM RED-HANDED SELLING STUFF TO SOMEONE ELSE.

> BETWEEN YOU AND MICHAEL, YOU'VE CERTAINLY CAUSED A FUSS! AND SOPHIE'S FRIEND, JANINE WAS CAUTIONED. WHAT A MESS!

> IT SURE IS. I NEVER THOUGHT THINGS WOULD TURN OUT LIKE THIS. I'M GOING TO GET BACK TO FITNESS AGAIN, THOUGH, AND TRY TO PERSUADE COACH TO LET ME BACK IN THE CLUB.

▽ At school a few days later, Kelly, Susan and the others were discussing what had happened.

> IT'S REALLY MADE ME THINK. A FEW MONTHS AGO, I WAS READY TO EXPERIMENT WITH THINGS. AFTER ALL THAT'S HAPPENED, I'M NOT SO SURE ANY MORE. THE RISKS ARE TOO HIGH.

> TOO RIGHT. HOW'S MICHAEL DOING?

> HE DIDN'T STOP TO THINK ABOUT WHAT WOULD HAPPEN. HE JUST HAD HIS EYES SET ON WINNING HIS RACE. HE'S LUCKY HE WASN'T SUSPENDED. DAD'S BEING QUITE SUPPORTIVE THOUGH.

△ Bruno said he thought it would still take a while for everyone at the club to trust him again.

> MUCH BETTER NOW. HE AND SOPHIE ARE GOING TO A GROUP FOR PEOPLE WHO'VE HAD DRUG PROBLEMS. IT'S REALLY SCARY. YOU DON'T EXPECT STUFF LIKE THIS TO HAPPEN TO PEOPLE YOU KNOW.

> OUR WHOLE FAMILY'S BEEN AFFECTED BY WHAT HAPPENED TO PHILIP.

> I'VE HEARD PEOPLE SAY SOME PRETTY NASTY THINGS.

> THINGS WILL GET BETTER. HE AND BRUNO ARE MATES AGAIN.

> WELL, WE ALL KNOW THE RISKS ARE REAL NOW, DON'T WE?

FACTFILE:
SAYING NO

Many anti-drug messages advise you to simply say no if you are offered drugs. But it is rarely that easy to say no.

- The best way to avoid having to say no, is not to put yourself in potentially difficult situations.
- Remember that people may try to persuade you. Try to stick to the same answer, without going into detail. People will often become bored with hearing you say the same thing again and again.
- Make clear statements, and try to say things like 'I won't' rather than 'I shouldn't' – don't give others a way in to try to persuade you.
- Walk away if they keep trying to persuade you or threaten you.
- Remember that it takes courage to stand up and say no to something that is illegal and unhealthy.
- If you are worried about a situation, speak to an adult who can help you with your concerns.

WHEN YOU ARE YOUNGER, IT CAN SEEM IMPOSSIBLE TO BELIEVE THAT ANYTHING YOU DO COULD HAVE A SERIOUS EFFECT ON YOUR FUTURE.

It can also be difficult to wait for something. But it is vital to think about the consequences of your actions – for you and for other people – and not to take stupid risks. Many young people have found that rushing into things without considering what the outcome might be has had very serious effects on their future life and health.

IT IS IMPORTANT TO KEEP THINGS IN PERSPECTIVE.

It may seem harmless to want to try out new things, but if experimenting means taking chances with your life and health it just isn't worth it. Talking about problems is one way of beginning to look for a solution. Speaking to someone you trust and being open and honest can help to clarify issues and ensure you know all of the facts about drug use and abuse.

What Can We Do?

"Once I realised that I didn't have to go through it alone, it was a lot easier to ask for help with the problem."

Having read this book, you will know more about some of the reasons people become involved with drugs and develop a drug problem. You should also understand some of the ways you can protect yourself and avoid situations in which you may be tempted to try drugs. Remember that all drugs have the potential to cause problems, both to your physical health and to your emotional and social well-being.

Good communication can help you to understand and explain emotions and sort out problems – even the most complex!

When growing up, it is important not to let your desire to try new things interfere with your judgement. Understanding the effects of drugs, and thinking out plans for refusing to go along with others if you are offered drugs, can help with this. If you are thinking about taking drugs, or have already experimented with them, you should consider why you are doing this, and think about the possible effects, not only on you, but on other people too. There really is a lot of help available. Adults can help too. Often, their behaviour can influence that of young people. If they see relatives smoking, drinking alcohol or using drugs illegally, young people might come to believe it is okay for them too.

Adults and young people who have read this book together might want to discuss their feelings about the issues raised. Anyone who would like to talk to someone not directly involved about drugs and drug abuse should be able to obtain help, support and advice from the organisations listed below.

NARCOTICS ANONYMOUS
P.O. BOX 1980
London, N19 3LS
Tel: 0171 272 9040
National Helpline:
Tel: 0171 498 9005
(10.00-22.00 hrs)

TURNING POINT
101 Back Church Lane
London, E1 1LU
Tel: 0171 702 2300

RELEASE – CRIMINAL, LEGAL AND DRUGS SERVICE
388 Old Street
London, EC1V 9LT
24 hour emergency helpline
Tel: 0171 603 8654

NATIONAL ALCOHOL HELPLINE
Tel: 0171 332 0150

THE INSTITUTE OF FAMILY THERAPY
43 New Cavendish Street
London, W1M 7RG
Tel: 0171 391 9150

ALCOHOL CONCERN
Waterbridge House
32-36 Loman Street
London, SE1 0EE
Tel: 0171 928 7377

ADFAM
18 Hatton Place
London, EC1N 8ND
Tel: 0171 405 3923

INSTITUTE FOR THE STUDY OF DRUG DEPENDENCE (ISDD)
Waterbridge House
32-36 Loman Street
London, SE1 0EE
Tel: 0171 928 1211

RE-SOLV
30 a High Street
Stone
Staffordshire, ST15 8AW
Tel: 01785 817885

FAMILIES ANONYMOUS
Unit 37
Doddington and Rollo
Community Association
Charlotte Despard Avenue
London
SW11 5JE
Tel: 0171 498 4680

ALCOHOL AND DRUG FOUNDATION (ADFA)
P.O. BOX 269
Woden, Act 2606
Australia

CHILDREN'S PROTECTION SOCIETY, AUSTRALIA
Tel: 00 613 458 3566

Index

Photocredits

All the pictures in this book are by Roger Vlitos, apart from 1 & 6 – Frank Spooner Pictures; 5 – Eye Ubiquitous; 11b – Rex Features. The publishers wish to acknowledge that all the people photographed in this book are models.